CHOICE IS YOURS

WHICH CHOICE DO YOU WANT TO MAKE

DEEP RANA

"To my coach, whose wisdom has shaped my journey—thank you for teaching me that consistency is powerful when fueled by love, and that every choice we make shapes the life we live. May this book remind us all that our daily decisions, big or small, define the paths we walk...."

Contents

Contents

Foreword

FOREWORD

life is like a game—you're constantly making moves, deciding which path to take, and shaping who youbecome. Every choice, big or small, has the power to shift your reality. Some days, you're choosing between growth and comfort. Other days, between feeling deeply or brushing it off like nothing happened.

That's what Choice is Yours is about. It's not a rulebook—it's a reminder that you're in control. You get to decide whether you level up, stay stuck, or rewrite the story entirely. Do you embrace emotions and use them as fuel, or do you let them weigh you down? Do you become the best version of yourself, or do you settle for "just okay"?

At the end of the day, your life is built on the choices you make. No pressure—just the freedom to decide. And the best part? The choice is always yours.

DEEP RANA

Preface

"We are our choices." – Jean-Paul Sartre

Every single day, you make choices. Some seem tiny—what to eat, how to start your morning. Others feel bigger—how you handle stress, whether you chase your dreams or stay in your comfort zone. But here's the thing: even the smallest choices stack up and shape the person you become.

Choice is Yours isn't here to tell you what to do. It's here to show you that you hold the power. It's about seeing life through a lens of growth, where every decision—how you think, how you feel, how you act—can be a step forward. Some days, that choice is about pushing yourself. Other days, it's about giving yourself grace. But no matter what, it's always yours to make.

"Between stimulus and response, there is a space. In that space is our power to choose our response." – Viktor Frankl

This book is an invitation to slow down, to become aware of the power in everyday moments, and to start making choices that bring you closer to the best version of yourself. Whether it's choosing patience over frustration, action over excuses, or self-belief over doubt—each moment is a chance to level up.

So here's to the power of choice. Here's to seeing things differently. And here's to you—becoming who you're meant to be, one decision at a time.

Because in the end, the choice is—and always will be—yours.

DEEEP RANA

Acknowledgements

To everyone who's ever stood at a crossroads, map in one hand and a wild dream in the other—this book is for you. A huge thanks to my coach, whose wisdom and encouragement reminded me that choices feel e ortless when they come from love. Your guidance has been a compass on this journey. To my circle of cosmic co creators: the friends who reminded me that no choice is fi nal, the family who cheered eve my weirdest decisions, and the mentors who taught me that the only wrong choice is not making one—thank you. And to the universe, the ultimate partner in this dance of decision,making—thank you for the synchronicities, the detours, and the quiet nudges to keep moving forward. Finally, to you, dear reader—thank you for choosing this moment to join me on this journey. Here's to the magic in every decision, the coolness of owning your pathTo everyone who's ever stood at a crossroads, map in one hand and a wild dream in the other—this book is for you. A huge thanks to my coach, whose wisdom and encouragement reminded me that choices feel e ortless when they come from love. Your guidance has been a compass on this journey. To my circle of cosmic cocreators: the friends who reminded me that no choice is fi nal, the family who cheered eve my weirdest decisions, and the mentors who taught me that the only wrong choice is not making one—thank you. And to the universe, the ultimate partner in this dance of decision making—thank you for the synchronicities, the detours, and the quiet nudges to keep moving forward. Finally, to you, dear reader—thank you for choosing this moment to join me on this journey. Here's to the magic in every decision, the coolness of owning your path.

Prologue

every day, from the moment we wake up, we are faced with choices. Some seem small—what to wear, whether to hit snooze, what to say in a conversation. Others feel bigger—whether to chase a dream, let go of the past, or take a step toward something unknown. But what if I told you that every choice, no matter how small, has the power to shape who you become?

Life isn't about having all the answers. It's about recognizing that you hold the pen in your own story. Your choices build your mindset, define your path, and create the person you see in the mirror. Even the simplest decision—whether to see a setback as an ending or a lesson—can change everything.

This book isn't here to preach or throw in a "10-step formula to success." Let's be real—that stuff sounds cool but rarely works. Instead, Choice is Yours is an invitation to see life differently—to realize that self-improvement, emotional balance, and growth don't come from luck; they come from the choices you make every single day.

So, before you move on, here's a thought:

? "Life is basically just a series of 'Should I eat this or not?' and 'Was that a bad decision?' moments."

? "Your comfort zone is like your bed—warm, cozy, and hard to leave. But nothing exciting happens if you stay in it all day."

? "At the end of the day, your choices shape your story. So, make it one worth reading."

Now, let's dive in. And remember—the choice is yours.

1

what's wrong with me, about what i feel?

———❤———

What's Wrong with Me? Sometimes, life feels like one giant emotional rollercoaster—and not the fun kind with cotton candy and excitement, but the kind where your seatbelt is loose, and you're just hanging on for dear life. You get sad about being sad, feel guilty about feeling guilty, and then angry because, well, why do emotions have to be so exhausting? And let's not even get started on the guilt spiral: "Why am I like this? Why can't I just chill? " But you know what? There's nothing actually wrong with us. Feeling all these emotions isn't a malfunction; it's being human. Think of it this way: emotions are like pop-up ads in your brain. Annoying, yes, but they're trying to get your attention. The key is to stop clicking "close" without reading the message. Next time you feel sad, instead of spiraling into, "Why am I so broken?" try asking, "Okay, what's going on here? Why am I sad?" It's like being your own detective—but instead of solving crimes, you're solving yourself. Spoiler alert: the culprit is usually something simple, like unmet expectations, overthinking, or the fact that someone nished your snack without asking. Here's the thing: emotions aren't trying to ruin your day; they're trying to tell you something. Sadness might be saying, "Hey, take a break." Anger might mean, "Set some boundaries!" Guilt might be a gentle nudge to refl ect not a hammer to beat yourself up with. Of course, we all have those days when our inner dialogue is less wise guru and more unhinged stand-up comedian. You tell yourself, "It's fine; I'll figure it out." But deep down, you're just waiting for someone to hand you a guidebook titled How to Be a Functional Human. (Spoiler: no one has that guidebook, not even the person who looks like they have it all together.) And let's be honest: sometimes, the best thing you can do is laugh at yourself. You're feeling sad? Fine, have a good cry, but also put on a ridiculous sitcom and laugh at something stupid. Angry at yourself? Go punch a pillow and then eat a snack like the drama queen you are. Life is chaotic, and that's okay. The magic happens when you stop judging yourself for feeling. Instead, lean into the messiness. Let sadness teach you patience, let guilt help you grow, and let anger push you toward what matters. But most importantly, remember: this too shall pass. You've survived every bad day so far, and you'll survive this one too. So next time your brain throws you into the emotional washing machine, take a breath. Say to yourself, "I'll figure it out, eventually. But for now? Let's embrace the chaos." And if you need a pick-me-up, just remember: everyone's a little messy. That's what makes us interesting. "

2

not every voice deserves a response. Protect your energy, ignore the noise, and keep going

One of the most negative effects on your journey comes from trying to change yourself to what others expect. Let's face it: people always have opinions, and trust me, they're not shy about sharing them. But if you're constantly tuning into everyone's station, you'll miss your own music. When you know your destination, your goal, there will always be people waving red flag and shouting, "You can't do that!" Guess what? You don't have to RSVP to every argument or listen to every critic in the peanut gallery. When you're on your path and faced with a thousand opinions — some cheering, some jeering — remember that your opinion about yourself is the VIP ticket. Sure, some people may try to shame you, embarrass you, or drag you down, but that's their problem, not yours. The trick? Mastering the art of ignoring. Ignorance isn't just bliss; it's your best defense against negativity. It's not about being rude; it's about keeping your energy sacred. Here's the thing: ignoring isn't a one-time superpower move. It's a daily skill — like brushing your teeth or charging your phone. Every day, you have to choose to tune out the noise and stay focused on your grind. It's like this: you can't run a race if you're stopping every seconds to argue with people on the sidelines. You've got to keep moving forward. Their opinions aren't paying your bills or chasing your dreams, so why let them rent space in your head? So, do what you want, how you want, and don't let anyone's judgment slow you down. Life's too short to worry about what someone who barely knows you thinks. Remember, stepping forward often means leaving behind the weight of other people's opinions. It's not just important; it's essential. Be cool, be confident, and let your vibe d the talking while you keep walking. This version blends humor, coolness, and motivation while emphasizing the importance of ignoring negativity to move forward.

3

Being a 14-year-old girl living in a hostel comes with its own set of challenges—like juggling my dreams, navigating society's endless rules, and dealing with constant judgment. Society loves to tell girls how to act, what to wear, and who to talk to. Honestly, it feels like a full-time job just living up to everyone's expectations. Take sports, for example. I'm out there giving my all, focused on the game, and bam—another proposal. I'm 14 and already had 18 of them! Seriously, can a girl not chase goals without someone thinking it's an open invite? My reaction? A mix of rolling my eyes and laughing it on because, hey, 'I'm not looking for a soulmate ; I'm looking for a win! But let's be real: this isn't just about sports—it's about how society puts boundaries on us. And sure, boys have their own challenges, but I can't speak for them because I'm not one. All I know is that as a girl, we're expected to follow these unspoken rules, and when we don't, the judgment comes ying Thankfully, I have my coach. They're like my secret weapon— someone I can share everything with, even stu I wouldn't tell my mom. They remind me that boundaries aren't bad;

they're empowering. Setting limits doesn't mean I'm weak—it means I know my worth. And that's a lesson I hold close: 'Your boundaries defi ne your strength not your limits. ' So now, I've made peace with this: I can't change society overnight, but I can control how I respond. Whether it's ignoring unsolicited attention, standing up for myself, or just staying focused on my goals, I'm learning every day. To the boys? You have your own struggles, and I respect that. But for now, I'm sticking to what I know—and what I know is this: girls deserve the space to grow, thrive, and set their own rules, no matter what society says.

4

what i belive is "If you don't grab the wheel, who will? Don't let life drive itself—you'll end up wherever it feels like going!"

"Sometimes, we know we're on the wrong path, but we still keep walking, thinking, 'Chal raha hai, toh chalne do.' But one day, I realized—if I keep owing with th crowd, I'll end up nowhere special. because " winner donot do diffrent things they do things diffrently" by shiv khera So, I decided to switch things up. Tiny changes became my secret weapon. Waking up at 4:30 a.m.? on sundays following my meditation routine .this give a little old vibes but it's important. Not exactly the dream. I'd tell myself, 'Just 5 more minutes!' every morning like a broken alarm clock. But then I thought, if I keep snoozing, I'm also snoozing on my goals. That's when I turned to Atomic Habits and my coach, who said, 'Take small steps, celebrate the wins, and keep moving forward.' And guess what? They were right. I started with baby steps— a rmations, a simple inhale exhale routine, and some stretching. My mantra? 'Slow progress is still progress, and at least I'm lapping everyone still sleeping!' Of course, there were days when I felt like a sleepy child and just wanted to Netfl ix my life away. But I remembered: 'Consistency beats motivation, and showing up is half the battle.' I'd slip, but I always stood back up because every time I did, I was building something bigger—myself. So, here's my vibe now: 'If you can't do it all, just do something small, but keep showing up.' Shoutout to my coach, my inner determination, and James Clear's Atomic Habits—turns

out, they're the dream team I never knew I needed!" The best time to prepare yourself? It's not now—it's that moment when everything feels like it's falling apart. When you're angry, sad, or just downright frustrated— that's your cue to level up. Trust me, I've been there. One day, I felt like a crumpled leaf in the wind—completely out of control. My coach asked what was wrong, and I pulled the classic 'stomach ache' excuse. Truth? I wasn't physically sick; I was emotionally drained. I was stuck in this loop of sadness and frustration, thinking, 'Why can't I just keep it together like everyone else?' But here's the plot twist: I realized that waiting to feel "better" wasn't the answer. If I wanted to control my emotions, I had to start right then. My coach gave me a gem of advice: 'When you feel like you're about to lose it, that's the perfect time to nd yourself' At first, it felt impossible. I'd get angry and snap, or feel sad and sulk like a toddler whose candy got stolen. But then I thought: If I can control myself in these moments, I can handle anything. Slowly, I started practicing— whether it was during games, tough conversations, or just those random bad days. And hey, it worked! Sure, I'm still a work in progress, but here's the funny part: 'I don't control my emotions because I'm Zen—I do it because I'm tired of apologizing for the things I said when I was hangry!' Now, every time things get tough, I remind myself: 'The extra mile doesn't have track—it's where the magic happens. ' And guess what? I'm getting better, one messy moment at a time.

5

"Your emotions are like a playlist—don't let one sad song be on repeat forever."

my coach always says" having emotions or being emotional have a huge diffrence . choice is yours what you want to have. this is something i never understand until i have experience it.or how imortant it is. She was a good friend of mine, and I could feel her wounds deeply. She was someone who always cared for me, but it became overwhelming. She didn't want me to me . who i am No doubt she cared for me, but it was more than that—she needed something beyond friendship. She thought her emotional dependence on me was justified but it wasn't. It may sound harsh, but I didn't like her being with me all the time. She used to bring chocolates for me, sleep by my side, and do silly things I never liked. We never fully connected, but I got stuck. She just wanted to spend every moment with me, talking, sharing, or staying close. But when I tried to distance myself, she would hurt herself. She once beat herself and claimed that, as her best friend, I was responsible. I didn't like that she was harming herself because of me but thats not my fault, so I tried to end things. But she didn't take it well—she even tried to cut her veins. She would make threats, like harming others or herself, if I refused to stay with her. I tried to get away from her, but it was diffcult. The emotional burden left me drained. Eventually, I shared everything with my mother about what was happening.I had to tell someone, so I confi ded in my mother "This isn't friendship , " this is just a foolishness of mine that i can't say 'no' to this rubbish I told her. "This is emotional blackmail. And I don't know how to escape it. " My mother listened, her face a mixture of concern and understanding. She held my hand and said, "Sometimes, you have to choose your own peace, even if it breaks someone else's heart. Her words gave me strength, but the scars of that time still linger. It was a lesson I never wanted to learn, yet one I'll never forget; this not end here but i am prepared for it.But i will didn't forget how much I struggled emotionally. How much I was confused, how much I doubted myself, and how much of it all was because of me. I've always been too emotional— always letting my heart speak louder than my mind. And maybe, just maybe, that's where it all went wrong. "We can't change ourselves completely, " I thought. "But at some point, we need to learn. Being emotional isn't a weakness, but letting it control you—letting it drown you—is. " and after that my mother told my teacher and she told her parent all the shit she was doing then her parents let herleft the school. and that seem that all because of me . my emotionalness . but no one is there to handle me in hostel . my mother also dont know how much i am storm I was facing inside. She thought I was ne on the surface but deep down, I was breaking. I didn't know how to handle how i feel and I didn't know how to handle myself. I was torn between trying to making myself feel better and losing myself in the process. she used to do hundreds of messages to my mother like "why do you don't allow me to talk to her" . The weight of those words crushed me. I kept asking myself, "How did we get here? Was it my fault? Did my constant emotional openness make her believe I could fix everything?" And maybe it was my fault. I let myself be too vulnerable, too accessible, and too involved. "You can't pour from an empty cup, " I whispered to myself one night, but by then, it was too late. I was drained. thing even dont end here the worst part when you loved one act like the biggest ignorer. My mother, the one person who believed in me the most, started questioning me. "This is your mistake, " she said. "You should've spoken up. You should've told someone—anyone—who could help. " Her words stung because they were true. I had let my emotions take over. I thought I could handle everything on my own, but I was wrong only my emotionalness ,attachment for her keep me away to tell someone. Even my friends, the ones who were always there for me, left. "You chose her over us, " they said. "And now you want us back?" I had no answer. How could I explain that I wasn't choosing her? I was just lost in a mess I didn't know how to clean up.My coach, who means so much to me— almost like my father, brother, or even a god-like gure—once tol me, "It's not your fault. " However, for months (around 5–6 months), I felt left out and burdened because no one shared or confinded in me. I felt isolated in my classes, hostel, and almost everywhere I went. I couldn't control *my emotions, and there was no one I could rely on. At first, I replaced my longing fo connection with expectations that someone—any loved one—might understand me. But no one did. Eventually, I told myself, "I'm here for myself. " I began to rebuild myself by focusing on useful tools, making new friends, and pursuing activities like reading. Slowly, things started to change. However, there were still moments that hurt the most. For instance, when she used to send me messages, but now those are blocked. She once told me that no one can hurt you when i am here for you, but it didn't happen. For a long time, I felt angry, betrayed, and upset, but I controlled myself. I decided I wasn't going to be a fool who lingered in the past. These experiences, though painful, taught me valuable lessons about persistence, failure, and self-reliance. They also became an important part of my journey. I remember one particular day—I was so excited and happy as we prepared for our tournament. During breakfast, someone told me, she is calling you. " For a moment, I froze. Then I saw her standing nearby, but I ignored her completely throughout the tournament. During our match, I noticed she was standing by the goalpost, not too far away. Despite that, we lost —not because of her, but She looked at me, and But through these ups and downs, I've learned to stay strong and focused. I now realize that moving forward is the only way to truly grow. Now, as I sit here reflecting everything, one thought keeps circling in my mind: "I let my emotions control me, and I let her take advantage of that. " But I've learned one thing through all of this: "Being emotional isn't a sin, but letting it blind you is sin and thats the best part I realized that this is the best and important part to lose my emotionalness .that pain hurts the most but the important one. I decided I wasn't going to be a fool who lingered in the past. These experiences, though painful, taught me valuable lessons about persistence, failure, and self-reliance. They also became an important part of my journey ' But through these ups and downs, I've learned to stay strong and focused. I now realize that moving forward is the only way to truly grow. and one thing more i am ready for every pain which makes me strong day by day i welcome every pain . please come bro you are my friend.*

6

The mind is still like a child, but if you understand it right, it can become your best ally. ")

Sometimes we let this thing called "mann" (our whims) control us. You know the feeling — when your mind says, "Yaar, I don't feel like it, " and suddenly, everything feels impossible. Exercise? Nah, the bed is calling. Studying? Meh, Netflex looks better. But here's the question: who's in charge here, you or this so-called mann? As my coach always says, consistency is key, but only when you truly love what you're doing. The Bhagavad Gita says that mann is our sarthi — our charioteer. It can either drive us to greatness or keep us stuck. The choice is yours. Think about it — how often do you skip something important just because you "don't feel like it"? Why is it so easy to choose the shortcut, even when we know what's better for us? The truth is, controlling your mann isn't about waiting for motivation; it's about showing up, even when you'd rather not. Let's get real: doing the hard things, the boring things, isn't fun at first. But ask yourself: why does it feel so awkward to try new habits or stick to a plan? The answer is simple — because you're not used to it. It's like trying to lift weights at the gym without practice — your muscles aren't ready yet, but with consistency, they grow. And yes, it's okay to feel like quitting when you don't see results right away. But here's the trick: start asking yourself the right questions. "What will happen if I stick with this?" or "Why am I letting temporary feelings decide my future?" When you challenge your mann instead of blindly following it, you take back control. So, the next time your mann whispers, "Let's just skip this, " you reply: "Nah, not today. I'm the boss here. " It's not about ghtin your mind all the time — it's about gently guiding it toward what you know is best. Keep showing up, keep doing the work, and watch how your mann learns to follow you instead. This includes the teachings of your coach and the Bhagavad Gita, emphasizing the importance of mann as a guide. Let me know if this feels right!

7

the mirror of better me with broken promises"

Let's be honest—building habits is like trying to train a cat to fetch. It sounds good in theory, but in practice? Chaos. That's exactly how I felt when I decided to "get serious" about life as a teenager. Take waking up early. It's the ultimate cliché for self improvement. I'd set my alarm for 5 AM, imagining myself as one of those tness infl uencers w meditate with sunrise. Day one, I nailed it. By day three, I was negotiating with my alarm: "If I skip breakfast, I can sleep for 20 more minutes. Deal?" My brain even threw in excuses like, "It's Sunday! Rest is self-care!" Spoiler alert: I overslept. Then there's the whole "plan your day" routine. Inspired by motivational quotes like "Failing to plan is planning to fail," I went all in. Every night, I'd sit down with my notebook, writing out my goals: Wake up early, study hard, avoid distractions. But many a time, I'd break those promises to myself faster than you can say "gossips." Living in a hostel added to the challenge. Hostel life is like living in a 24/7 sitcom—there's always something happening. Gossip sessions, heated debates over who's the best football player, late-night movie marathons—it's impossible to resist. Amid all this chaos, sticking to a routine felt like mission impossible. Enter my coach, the unsung hero of my life. He saw me struggling and pulled me aside one day. "Habits are like planting seeds," he said. "You won't see the results immediately, but if you keep watering them, one day, you'll have a tree." His words hit me harder than a football to the face. He didn't just talk about discipline; he lived it. Watching him lead by example made me realize that habits aren't about perfection—they're about persistence.

He taught me that even small steps count, as long as you keep moving forward. One of his favorite lines was, "If you can't do it perfectly, do it anyway. Progress, not perfection, is the goal." Motivated by his words, I revamped my approach. I started reflecting on my day—not t criticize myself but to learn. What went well? What didn't? How could I improve? I also found ways to stay grounded, like reading a page of the Bhagavad Gita or having meaningful conversations with friends. Of course, I still stumbled. There were days when my resolve crumbled, and I'd wander o during a free period, convincing myself that roaming around the campus was "networking." My coach would catch me and give me that look. You know the one—the "You can do better than this" look. But instead of scolding me, he'd remind me: "Discipline isn't about never failing; it's about bouncing back every time you do." Over time, I realized he was right. Habits are built one small step at a time. Waking up early, planning my day, staying consistent—it's not about getting it right every single day. It's about showing up, even when it's hard. Now, whenever I feel like giving up, I think of my coach's words: "The hardest part is starting. Once you do, momentum will take care of the rest." And you know what? He was right. So here's to the messy, hilarious, and rewarding journey of building habits. If I, with all my teenage drama and broken promises, can make progress, so can you. Remember: "Great things are not done by impulse, but by a series of small things brought together."

8

love the process...............

The Art of Falling in Love with the Process Embrace the journey, not just the destination. There's something magical about the process—the messy middle that most people rush through. I get it, at rst, it feels like a grind Whether you're living in a hostel, writing a book, or just navigating life, it's all a lot to handle. But here's the truth: you don't have to love it right away. You just have to let yourself feel it. And as my coach always says: "Consistency is key—but only if you love doing it." I wasn't always into this whole "embrace the process" thing. It felt like work, and work feels like something to avoid. But then I realized—it's not about getting to the end. It's about learning to vibe with the ow, even when it' messy In the beginning, you'll ask yourself, "Why am I doing this?" But over time, it shifts. It becomes more like a rhythm, a song where you create your own beats. You can't just skip to the good part; you have to enjoy the verses, even if they're slow. The beauty is in the struggle, the tiny steps that make up the bigger picture. Chillness in the Chaos Living in a hostel can feel like chaos sometimes, right? But you can't ght it—you've got to ride it The real trick is learning to chill, knowing that not everything needs to be perfect. No one expects you to have it all gured out. So take breath, let go of the stress, and remember that it's all part of the ride. Celebrate the small wins— making your bed, nishing a page or even just getting through the day. The little things add up. "Love the grind, but don't let it grind you down. " The key is ndin that balance between consistency and enjoying what you're doing. If you hate the grind, you won't stick with it. But if you love it, you won't even notice the e ort. That's where the magic happens. Turning the Struggle into the Dance There are days when it feels like you're stuck in the same loop, but those days are part of your growth. Don't rush them. Think of it like dancing. You can't just jump to the fun part; you need to feel the rhythm. When life throws you a curveball, all you need to do is roll with it, stay . Every struggle i just another step in your own dance. "It's not about being perfect; it's about being present. " The process isn't something you do—it's something you become. You start to notice the small, beautiful changes: the way you handle stress, how you improve each day, how you grow in ways you didn't expect. You're not just doing the work, you're becoming the person who loves the work. And that's where the real transformation happens. The Power of Consistency and Love "Consistency is important—but only when you love what you're doing. " My coach's words ring true: consistency won't feel like a burden if you're genuinely into it. When you love something, the act of doing it becomes e ortless. Every task, no matter how repetitive, feels more like an opportunity than a chore. "The process is the prize. " There's no magic formula, no secret shortcut. It's all about showing up every day, nding your groove, an enjoying the ride. Your success is in your daily choices, your ability to keep going, even when it feels like you're not getting anywhere. Eventually, you'll look back and realize just how far you've come. So here's to the process. Here's to consistency, to the little victories, to the grind that becomes a ow Here's to falling in love with the journey, to chilling through the chaos, and knowing that every step is part of something bigger. "Keep going. The process is the place where your magic happens. " And when in doubt: Chill, trust the process, and let it love you back

9

SOME PERSONAL TALK

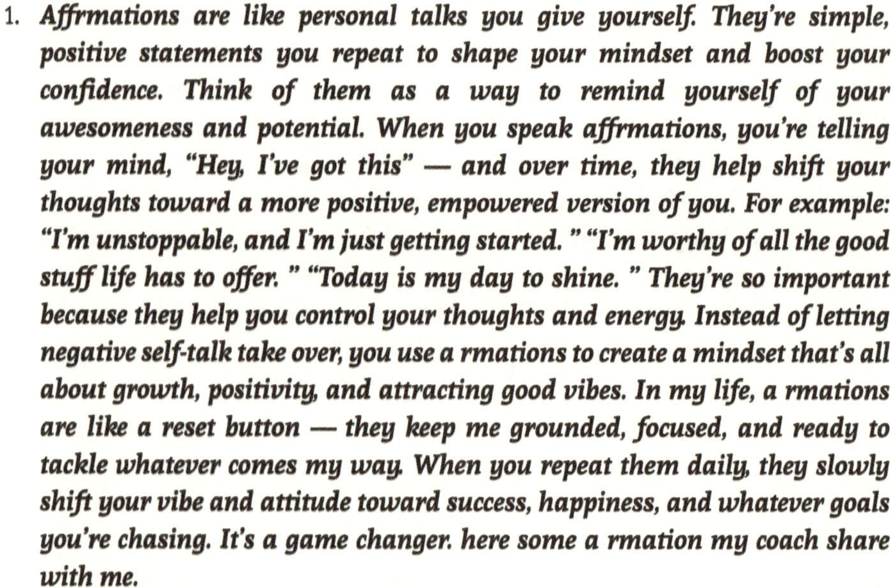

1. *Affirmations are like personal talks you give yourself. They're simple, positive statements you repeat to shape your mindset and boost your confidence. Think of them as a way to remind yourself of your awesomeness and potential. When you speak affirmations, you're telling your mind, "Hey, I've got this" — and over time, they help shift your thoughts toward a more positive, empowered version of you. For example: "I'm unstoppable, and I'm just getting started." "I'm worthy of all the good stuff life has to offer." "Today is my day to shine." They're so important because they help you control your thoughts and energy. Instead of letting negative self-talk take over, you use a rmations to create a mindset that's all about growth, positivity, and attracting good vibes. In my life, a rmations are like a reset button — they keep me grounded, focused, and ready to tackle whatever comes my way. When you repeat them daily, they slowly shift your vibe and attitude toward success, happiness, and whatever goals you're chasing. It's a game changer. here some a rmation my coach share with me.*

- *I step into this day with calm and peace*
- *. I begin my day radiating positive energy.*
- *I dive into today with optimism and excitement.*
- *Today, I attract abundance effortlessly.*
- *Today, prosperity ows to me i magical ways.*
- *Today, life surprises me with beautiful moments.*
- *I am open to the serendipity of chance encounters.*
- *This day is a miracle unfolding.*

- *9. Today is one-of-a-kind, made just for me.*
- *This is a day unlike any other, filled with endless possibilities*
- *1. I celebrate life in all its glory today.*
- *I honor the infi nite intelligenc of the universe.*
- *Today is another chance to love, live, and serve with joy.*
- *. Today is truly a wonderful day.*
- *. I overflow with boundles energy today.*
- *. My excitement for today knows no limits.*
- *. I carry a sense of anticipation for the magic today brings.*
- *. Today is my day to shine brightly and confidently .*
- *I take inspired action today to make my dreams real.*
- *Today, I leave a mark with my impact and energy.*
- *. This is a day filled with amazing opportunities.*
- *. I am present, here, and fully alive today.*
- *I ow with flexibility and ea today.*
- *. I am solution-focused, overcoming challenges with grace.*
- *. I choose to feel amazing today.*
- *. I express my joy, letting it spread to everyone around me.*
- *I laugh freely and easily today.*
- *. Happiness is my choice today, and I embrace it fully.*
- *Today, I nd beauty an goodness in unexpected places.*
- *I experience joy, even when it comes out of nowhere.*
- *This day is truly amazing, just as it is.*
- *Today is full of limitless potential and adventure.*
- *I am so grateful for another chance to experience life in all its beauty.*
- *I eagerly discover what today has in store for me.*
- *Today is already shaping up to be an incredible day.*
- *The universe is brimming with possibilities for me today.*
- *What wonderful surprises await me today?*
- *I begin this day with an open heart, ready for anything.*
- *My mind is open and ready for all the new ideas that will come my way.*
- *. I can't wait to uncover the delightful treasures waiting for me today.*
- *. My energy is high as I embrace this wonderful day.*
- *. Yes, today is definitely fantastic day!*
- *. I am so thankful for the abundance in my life.*
- *Today, I recognize the many blessings I've been given.*
- *. Gratitude lls me, propellin me to attract even more positivity.*
- *This is an absolutely fabulous day.*

- *I feel alive, awake, and aware of all the beauty around me today.*
- *. Confidence flows through today.*
- *I embody success in everything I do today.*
- *I express my joy and passion freely today.*
- *. Oh yes, today is truly an amazing day.*
- *I bask in the glow of contentment and peace.*
- *I am uplifted, fulfi lled, an feeling so alive.*
- *I am on purpose today, moving toward my dreams.*
- *Today is the perfect day to live with passion and intensity.*
- *Clarity and focus ow throug me as I move through today.*
- *. This day is already wonderful, and I'm just getting started.*
- *Today, I choose love, compassion, and understanding.*
- *. I embody love in every interaction and every step I take.*
- *. This is an absolutely fabulous day.*
- *. This is a beautiful, joyful, funfilled day*
- *. Life feels amazing, and I am living it to the fullest.*
- *. I am lled with excitement gratitude, and peace today.*
- *This is a really, really good day – and it's only going to get better.*
- *. I am doing the best I can, and that's more than enough.*
- *I am worthy of all the love and success that ows into my life*
- *. It's okay to ask for help when I need it.*
- *I am capable of imagining things far beyond my limits.*
- *My boundaries are sacred, and I honor them.*
- *My feelings are important and deserve to be acknowledged.*
- *. It's okay to start over and try again – today is a fresh start.*
- *. I am allowed to say "No" when it feels right for me.*
- *. What others think of me doesn't define my worth*
- *. My peace is what matters most – and I protect it ercely*
- *I never expect anything from anyone – I create my own joy.*
- *Today, I am stronger and more resilient than yesterday.*
- *. I am ready for whatever today brings – I'm equipped for greatness.*
- *. I am safe and protected, surrounded by positive energy.*
- *.I welcome health, light, and peace into my life today.*
- *I am so inspired and ready to enjoy my day*

10

When you change for yourself, the vibe shifts, the energy hits, and everything starts to align.

Change yourself, but do it for yourself. No one, not even your mom, has the magical power to change you unless you decide you're ready. Some people might say, "Their love changed me," but let's be real — that change only happens when you're like, "Okay, I'm ready for a makeover!" It's not about waiting for some fairy tale romance to swoop in and fix you; it' about rolling up your sleeves and getting to work on your own life. And hey, if you don't want to change, that's fine too. Just don't expect anyone else to do the heavy lifting Love from others might inspire you, but the real change happens when you look in the mirror and say, "I'm awesome, and I'm going to be even awesomer." It's like trying to change the Wi-Fi password at someone's house — you can't do it unless you're the one with the access. Your power to transform your life is in your hands, not someone else's. So stop waiting for the "perfect moment" or that one person to swoop in and fix your problems. You're the hero o your own story — now go kick some butt. One of the best lessons I've gotten from my coach is this: consistency matters, but only if you actually enjoy what you're doing. Trying to stick to something you hate is like trying to wear shoes that are two sizes too small — you'll just end up with blisters and a lot of frustration. When you love what you're working on, that's when the real magic happens. And yes, sometimes the funniest questions are the ones that make you stop and think: "Wait... why didn't I think of that before?" It's like that moment when you realize you've been wearing your T-shirt inside out all day and only now, in front of a crowd, you realize... "Oops." So, embrace the journey, enjoy the laughs along the way, and remember: change yourself for YOU. Not because someone told you to. Not because you think it'll make you fit in. Bu because you're already pretty incredible, and you've just got to keep polishing that shine. Now there's a bit more humor and emotion woven through the message. It's lighthearted but still powerful! Let me know if you'd like more adjustments or if this hits the mark.

11

Sympathy is saying, 'Let me know if you need anything.' Empathy is showing up with ice cream and Netflix already cued up.

—♡—

" Empathy is the quiet ability to step into someone else's shoes, to truly feel what they're feeling. Sympathy, on the other hand, is standing on the outside, feeling sorry for someone but not really connecting with their pain. While we often talk about showing empathy to others, how often do we extend that same understanding to ourselves? The Pain of Being Overlooked Imagine this: You're angry and heartbroken because your most trusted friend let you down. You gave them your trust, your secrets, your everything, but they hurt you in ways you didn't expect. You sit alone, tears streaming down your face, feeling the weight of betrayal. You tell yourself, "No one cares about me, " and in your sadness, you skip meals, cry endlessly, and hope someone—anyone—will notice your pain and reach out. But no one does. You wait, silently pleading for your friend to show up, apologize, or at least ask if you've eaten. They don't. And you begin to spiral, telling yourself, "I'm not worth it." The Trap of Self-Sympathy In moments like this, we often fall into self-

sympathy. We pity ourselves, amplifying our hurt with thoughts like, "Why does this always happen to me? Why am I always alone?" It's a cycle that feeds on itself, leaving us stuck and drained. But here's the truth: No one can rescue you the way you can rescue yourself. Turning to Self-Empathy Now, imagine a di erent approach. Instead of wallowing in self-pity, try self-empathy. Pause and acknowledge your feelings: "I'm hurt, and it's okay to feel this way." Then, remind yourself that you deserve love and care—even if it comes from you. Instead of waiting for someone else to check on you, check on yourself. Make yourself a warm meal, wrap yourself in a cozy blanket, and whisper to yourself, "I've got this. I'll be okay." Treat yourself the way you wish your friend would have treated you. In doing so, you reclaim your power. You stop waiting for validation or comfort from others and start giving it to yourself. The Beauty of Self-Compassion This shift from self-sympathy to self-empathy is transformative. Instead of seeing yourself as a victim of life's circumstances, you become your own source of strength. You learn to stand tall, even in the face of heartbreak, because you know how to care for yourself. Here's another example: Imagine failing at something important—an exam, a project, or a goal you worked tirelessly for. The initial reaction is often harsh self criticism or drowning in pity: "I'm a failure. I'm not good enough." But what if, instead, you said, "I tried my best, and that's enough for now. I'll learn from this and come back stronger." Relatable Feelings We All Face We've all experienced moments of loneliness, rejection, or failure. It's easy to get stuck in self-sympathy, but it never leads to healing. Self empathy, on the other hand, allows you to acknowledge your pain while also nding a wa forward. It's the di erence between saying, "I'm broken, " and saying, "I'm healing." How to Practice Self-Empathy

1. Acknowledge Your Pain: Sit with your feelings. Don't dismiss them, but don't let them consume you either.

2. Be Kind to Yourself: Speak to yourself as you would to a dear friend. Replace harsh words with gentle ones.

3. Take Positive Actions: Even small steps—like eating, resting, or journaling—can show yourself love and care.

4. Let Go of Expectations: Stop waiting for others to x you Become your own source of comfort and strength. Final Thoughts (With a Twist) Life is tough, and heartbreak is inevitable. But the way you respond to your pain shapes your journey. Choosing self-empathy doesn't mean ignoring your emotions—it means embracing them while also nurturing yourself. When you learn to empathize with your own heart, you unlock a quiet strength that no one can take away. You stop being a prisoner of your pain and start becoming the architect of your healing. And remember: if all else fails, go buy yourself a tub of ice cream, turn on your favorite show, and tell yourself, "At least I don't have to share this ice cream with anyone!" Because, hey, self-care comes in many forms—even chocolate chip cookie dough

12

HeART- ' I am not beautiful ' MIND- you are you thats great. HEART- hmm...

———————♡———————

you are not beautiful, just your age to beautiful,

It doesnt matter how you look and what your skin colon

because everything change with age

At the end you need a holding hand, not a perfect body or a beautiful face.

in their own way not fat, slim, small, ugly black white

you are you and that s great.

when I heard this i just gone deeply in these words that just my age is beautiful not I . And understand that The time I waste looking in mirror thinking If I have better eyes or scrutinizing every detail, hoping to catch a glimpse of the "better" version of myself. This pursuit often feels like a waste of time, yet it's a habit that many of us have or to we dont want to change it to break. But why do i do it? foolish I am doing for just that one apperance that doesn't matter .i i i i know you too are one of them.that appearence waste your time thing about it. And some where binds you to not take a step forwards for your extramile. or binds you be confi dent who you look, be confident to not be perfect, or binds you to to always presentable. no need for that yaar.

13

what pain do you want to have in your lives?

Do we want pain in our lives?

Which type of pain?

If yes, no one wants pain in their life, but we all experience pain in the form of problems and challenges. Pain never lets you go; it stays with you unless you learn to manage it. The more pain you endure, the stronger you become. Imagine being someone who has faced pain since childhood and is now strong because of it. But what if someone you trust the most hurts you? Now you don't know how to react. Do you know what your condition will be? So, how important is pain? To be prepared for problems and pain, you must do things you don't want to do. This means preparing yourself for any situation. If you are an emotional person, and your emotions make you vulnerable to hurt, then you need to keep preparing yourself. Build challenges for yourself. If you get hurt easily, make a promise to yourself to not let others' actions a ect you too deeply.

14

what i think is not always right........

f

if I'm not good at my game, I think I can't do things right. I can't be a traveler if I'm right. Of course, many times when a ght happens we think that we are the only ones who are right. No matter if the fi ght is with ourselves or others, a times this mindset of always thinking we are right can break the most precious friendships and relationships. If you don't agree with me, just think about this: a person who is psychotic or has a bad mentality towards anything doesn't know what they are doing. They too think they are right. What holds us back is always thinking we are right . For example, a thought that always comes to my mind is: "Can I become a good psychologist?" or "My parents would never allow me to pursue this career, and it makes me feel sad. " But I question myself. What I thought was right may not be. Am I brave enough to tell my parents this? If I do, I know they won't agree. So, why I make myself feel bad. what if they agree with me. choice is mine if i want to question my self on what i think or just go with the ow of world tha i am the one who is right.so be careful what you think. and i want to tell you about i have read in the book subtile art of not giving fuck"that comedian Emo philips onces said, i used to think human brain was one of the wonderful organ in his body. then he realised who is telling me this. Learn from your mistakes and from others as well. Sometimes, we feel there is nothing to learn, thinking, "This isn't my fault, " or "There's nothing I could have done differently. " But the truth is, every experience holds a lesson, even if it doesn't seem obvious at rst For example, I failed to be a good helper. I saw myself as just average—like a goalkeeper who struggles to save balls. I practiced daily, but in matches, I couldn't perform well. Each failure made me doubt myself. I thought, "I'm not a good keeper, and I never will be." I worried about what others thought—my housemates and classmates laughed at my mistakes, and I felt embarrassed. But over time, I realized that failure is part of learning. From these experiences, I learned patience, resilience,

the importance of persistence. Here are a few key lessons:

1. Accepting Responsibility: Instead of blaming others or making excuses, I started focusing on what I could control. For example, during one match, I missed several saves and wanted to blame the team for poor coordination. But I realized my positioning and reflexes could improve, so worked harder on those aspects.

2. Practicing with a Purpose: It's not enough to just put in hours; you need to analyze and adjust. After struggling with saving low-angle shots, I began watching videos and seeking advice from better players. Slowly, I noticed improvement.

3. Handling Criticism: It's hard when people criticize or laugh at you. At rst, I felt crushe when classmates mocked me for missing easy saves. But now, I use their comments as motivation to prove myself.

4. Building Emotional Strength: I used to cry or feel defeated after every mistake. Now, I remind myself that setbacks are temporary. I look at failure as a stepping stone rather than a wall. 5. Recognizing Growth: Small improvements matter. For example, I managed to save a di cult shot in one match. Even though we didn't win, I felt proud because it showed my training was paying off. These lessons apply beyond just goalkeeping—they're about life. Whether it's academics, relationships, or personal goals, the principles remain the same. Hard work, patience, and learning from failure are what lead to success. Most importantly, I've learned not to let temporary opinions defi n my self-worth. People who laugh at you today won't matter tomorrow, but your growth and persistence will stay with you. Now, I focus on building my future, training myself to be mentally and physically strong. I'm learning to lter out negativity even if it comes from people I love, and channel it into selfimprovement. Success is not just about talent; it's about perseverance and the ability to rise every time you fall. so chill bro! now choice is mine i keep thinking what people will think or be happy let them think it's there work . and one thing more if they laugh on you so be happy someone laugh because of you.

15

choice is yours

in bagwat gita i read- "Life is full of ups and downs— successes and failures. But here's the thing: what happens to you doesn't defi ne you; how you respond to it does" . this tell me how we create difficulty by ou own. Every moment comes with a choice. Will you grow, or will you stay stuck? The choice is yours. Imagine this: You play a match, and it doesn't go as planned. Maybe you didn't practice enough, or maybe you gave it everything, but luck wasn't on your side. You could sit there thinking, "I'm just not good at this, " or, "This isn't my fault. " But does that help? Nope. Instead, you have to ask yourself: What am I going to do about it? Because, at the end of the day, the choice is yours. Excuses vs. Effort When life throws challenges your way, you're faced with two options:

1. Make excuses—blame bad luck, tough conditions, or someone else.

2. Take responsibility—learn, improve, and try again. Sure, you might get lucky once in a while, but luck isn't a strategy. If you want real growth, you've got to put in the work. It's not always easy, but guess what? The choice is yours. A Cool Lesson from My Principal One day, my principal said something in assembly that stuck with me: "You can tell someone a hundred good things about themselves, but the moment you criticize them once, that's all they'll remember. " Isn't that the truth? We're wired to focus on the negative—especially when it comes to ourselves. When people doubt you, gossip about you, or hurt you, it's easy to feel crushed. But here's a thought: you don't have to let their words control you. How you react is up to you. The choice is yours. Focus on What You Can Control Not everything in life is within your control. You can't change someone's opinion or force them to see your worth. What you can change is how you respond. Do you spend your energy trying to fix things that aren't fixable, or you focus on building yourself up? The choice is yours. This reminds me of a famous prayer:

"<u>God, grant me the serenity to accept the things I cannot change, the courage to change the things I can, and the wisdom to know the difference. </u>" <u>It's simple advice, but it's a game changer when you apply</u> it.

Stop Trying to Change People Here's a truth we all need to hear: You can't change people. You can't make them see things your way or act di erently just because you want them to. Someone who values you might change for the better, but only if they choose to. Instead of waiting for others to change, focus on yourself. Do you want to stay frustrated, or do you want to grow stronger? The choice is yours. Feeling Stuck Happens to Everyone Let's be real—sometimes life feels like you're running in circles. You're sad, frustrated, or just plain tired. Then you get mad at yourself for feeling that way, and it becomes a never-ending loop. But guess what? You're not alone. It happens to everyone. The key is to break free. Accept that some things are out of your hands. Ask yourself: Do you want to stay stuck, or do you want to move forward? Once again, the choice is yours. What Really Matters Here's the reality: Success and failure are both temporary. What matters is how you handle them. Do you let failure defi ne you, or d you use it as fuel to try again? Do you let success make you complacent, or do you keep striving? The choice is always yours. Final Thoughts with a Cool Twist Life isn't perfect, and that's okay. Some days you'll win, and some days you'll lose. But every experience teaches you something—if you're willing to learn. And when life gets tough, just remember this: "You can't control the wind, but you can adjust your sails—and maybe grab a snack while you're at it. Snacks fix everything. " Because at the end of the day, how you navigate the storm is up to you. The choice is yours.

16
what i feel

Life isn't just about ticking boxes like some pre-written script. School till 22, get a job by 25, settle down by 30, have kids, and then just wait till 60 for retirement? Nah, I'm not buying that. That's the life they want, but not the one I'm here to live. I've got bigger dreams. I want to travel the world, see every corner of it,oh you can say world is round but i will nd my own corner. meet d fferent people, and experience life in a way most only dream of. Why be stuck in one place when the world is out there waiting for you? I want to be a psychologist one day, not just studying minds, but helping people really understand themselves, their struggles, their dreams. Maybe I'll even open my own school where kids learn how to live — how to face life head-on, no matter what's thrown at them. None of this "get a good job and live happily ever after" nonsense. Society's mentality is the biggest joke — they say life is set once you fi nish school, get a good job, hav a happy family, then just wait till 60 to live. Seriously? Who came up with this? We're all supposed to live the same way, but that's not my path. It's not about doing what everyone else is doing. Life is about what you do with it. People can think what they want, but their opinions won't change my destiny. I want to wake up every day with purpose, not just drag myself through life hoping to make it to retirement. I'm gonna live now. Whether it's playing football or creating something that matters — I'll choose to live fully, on my own terms. People might say "don't take risks" or "follow the plan, " but I know the only risk is not living the life I want. At the end of the day, it's not about how long I live, but how much I live while I'm here. So, I'm choosing to make today count, not just wait for the "perfect time" that may never come. And trust me, this is my destination. What people think? Doesn't matter. I'm just here to live my life, on my terms, in my own cool, unapologetic way.

and you to have the way for your own life? just n it out . its never late and just explore your way no need to n hacks. just love the proces ..... you will get the way. graitefull for every thing . for pains, challanges because they make me strong. Life is about the choices we make, and one decision can change everything. some time these choices can be go in wrong way but its ok .For me, that decision was football .i am not good at it but what football teaches me no one else can. But it wasn't just about kicking a ball around; it was about discovering a path, a purpose, and a new way of seeing the world—all thanks to my coach. Before football, I felt like I was just going through the motions, not truly understanding my potential or the world around me. I grew up in a place where society didn't expect much from girls. Most believed we should become teachers or nurses—safe and respectable options, but nothing more. Dreams of leadership or athletic achievement were considered out of reach. Then I met my coach. From the moment I stepped onto the eld he saw something in me that I didn't even see in myself. "Football isn't just a game, " he said. "It's a way of life. It's about discipline, resilience, and learning to see the world through a di erent lens. " At first, I didn't fully understand what he meant. But as I trained, the lessons became clear. Every drill, every sprint, every match wasn't just about improving my skills—it was about building character. My coach taught me to embrace challenges, not fear them. He pushed me to think critically, to lead with confi dence and to always strive for more. Through football, I began to see life di erently. I realized that setbacks weren't failures; they were opportunities to grow. I learned that teamwork wasn't just about passing the ball but about supporting one another, both on and o the eld My coach didn't just teach me how to play; he taught me how to live. He believed in my dreams, even when others doubted them. He encouraged me to challenge the norms of my society, where girls were often held back by outdated expectations. "You're more than what they see, " he'd say. "Prove it to yourself first, an the world will follow. " Under his guidance, I began to thrive—not just as a player but as a person. Football became my passion, my sanctuary, and my teacher. It gave me the confi denc to dream bigger and the courage to chase those dreams. Today, I wake up every morning with gratitude. I thank God for giving me the strength to follow my path, and I thank my coach for showing me that path in the rs place. His lessons stay with me, both on and o the eld To anyone reading this: Find your passion, and when you do, nd mentor who can help you see your potential. Trust the journey, embrace the challenges, and never stop learning. Life isn't just about the destination—it's about the people and moments that shape who you become along the way.

thanks for reading my book....

About Author

A football-loving, psychology-obsessed, nature-admiring observer of life, DEEPIKA believes that the smallest choices shape the biggest moments. She's an average student by the numbers but a curious mind by nature, constantly exploring the way thoughts, emotions, and decisions create our reality.

Studying at Motilal Nehru Rai Sports School (and no, they don't pay for advertising!), she finds balance between the thrill of the game, the depth of psychology, and the quiet art of observing the world. Whether analyzing a match, unraveling the mysteries of human behavior, or simply watching the way leaves dance in the wind, she knows that every moment tells a story—if you pay attention.

Some words she lives by:

? "The mind is a playground. Play wisely."

? "Observation is the silent superpower."

? "Every small choice is a step toward who you're becoming."

? "Nature speaks. The question is—are you listening?"

THANKS TO MY COACH VK. DHAIYA,